U.S. SPECIAL OPS FORCES

INSIDE PARARESCUE

HOWARD PHILLIPS

PowerKiDS
press

NEW YORK

Published in 2022 by The Rosen Publishing Group, Inc.
29 East 21st Street, New York, NY 10010

First Edition

Editor: Greg Roza
Designer: Rachel Rising

Portions of this work were originally authored by Mark A. Harasymiw and published as *Pararescuemen*. All new material in this edition was authored by Howard Phillips.

Photo Credits: Cover, pp. 18, 19, 21, 23 Stocktrek Images/Getty Images; cover, pp. 1, 3–32 CRVL/Shutterstock.com; cover, p. 1 Zsschreiner/Shutterstock.com; cover, pp.1, 3, 30, 31, 32 Massimo Saivezzo/Shutterstock.com; p. 4 Sean Gladwell/Moment/Getty Images; pp. 5, 7, 11, 15, 19, 21, 25, 27 Khvost/Shutterstock.com; p. 5 NurPhoto/Contributor/Getty Images. p. 7 USAF/Handout/Getty Images News/Getty Images; p. 8 Three Lions/Stringer/ Hulton Archive/Getty Images; p. 9 Central Press/Stringer/Archive Photos/Getty Images; p. 11 Underwood Archives/Contributor/Archive Photos/Getty Images; p. 12 William MacKenzie/Contributor/Moment/Getty Images; p. 13 Ashley Cooper/The Image Bank Unreleased/Getty Images; p. 15 Nuk2013/Shutterstock.com; p. 16 VitaminCo/Shutterstock.com; p. 17 Bettmann/Contributor/Getty Images; p. 22 Joost Lagerweij/EyeEm/Getty Images; p. 25 HIGH-G Productions/Stocktrek Images/Getty Images; p. 27 https://en.wikipedia.org/wiki/File:Duane_hackney.jpg; p. 28 https://en.wikipedia.org/wiki/File:United_States_Air_Force_Pararescue_Emblem.svg; p. 29 U.S. Air Force/Handout/Getty Images News/Getty Images.

Some of the images in this book illustrate individuals who are models. The depictions do not imply actual situations or events.

Cataloging-in-Publication Data

Names: Phillips, Howard.
Title: Inside pararescue / Howard Phillips.
Description: New York : PowerKids Press, 2022. | Series: U.S. special ops forces | Includes glossary and index.
Identifiers: ISBN 9781725328853 (pbk.) | ISBN 9781725328877 (library bound) | ISBN 9781725328860 (6 pack)
Subjects: LCSH: United States. Air Force–Parachute troops–Juvenile literature. | United States. Air Force–Search and rescue operations–Juvenile literature. | Search and rescue operations–Juvenile literature. | Special forces (Military science)–United States–Juvenile literature.
Classification: LCC UG633.P54 2022 | DDC 358.4'141–dc23

Manufactured in the United States of America

CPSIA Compliance Information: Batch #BSPK22. For further information contact Rosen Publishing, New York, New York at 1-800-237-9932.

Find us on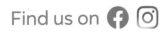

CONTENTS ⭐

AIR FORCE

The U.S. Air Force started as part of the army. In 1947, the United States recognized that airpower had become a major factor in modern conflicts and the air force needed to be an independent branch of the military.

The air force's mission is to fly and fight in air, space, and **cyberspace**. It uses highly trained pilots to fly planes to protect and support U.S. ground forces. The air force has many units of airmen working toward this mission. One of these units is known as pararescue. The brave airmen who join this unit are special operations service members.

PJs

THE AIRMEN WHO JOIN PARARESCUE ARE KNOWN AS
PARARESCUEMEN. THEY ARE ALSO CALLED PJs, WHICH
IS SHORT FOR PARAJUMPERS. THEY ARE SOME OF THE
MOST SKILLED AIRMEN IN THE WORLD. WHILE OTHER U.S.
SPECIAL FORCES UNITS—SUCH AS NAVY SEALS, ARMY
RANGERS, AND GREEN BERETS—ARE TRAINED TO LOCATE
AND ATTACK THE ENEMY, THE PJs' FIRST JOB IS TO HELP
DOWNED AIRMEN AND OTHER INJURED SOLDIERS.

THE AIR FORCE WAS FIRST PART OF THE U.S. ARMY.
IT WAS FIRST CALLED THE ARMY AIR CORPS.

PARAMEDICS IN COMBAT

Pararescue teams perform rescue operations, but they do much more than just that. They're emergency medical technicians (EMTs) and paramedics with a mission to search for and treat injured soldiers. They're trained to work in all kinds of conditions and handle many kinds of injuries—all while risking their lives.

PJs travel to their patients by airplane, helicopter, or parachute. They may even use diving gear if they have to rescue someone in the water! PJs are also trained in combat. Their missions may include fighting enemy soldiers, especially when it means protecting their patients in the field.

AIR FORCE SPECIAL OPS

THE BRANCH OF THE U.S. AIR FORCE RESPONSIBLE FOR OVERSEEING PJs, AS WELL AS OTHER AIR FORCE SPECIAL FORCES, IS THE AIR FORCE SPECIAL OPERATIONS COMMAND (AFSOC). AFSOC TROOPS ARE PART OF MANY MISSIONS. THEY HELP AIR FORCES IN OTHER COUNTRIES. THEY ALSO DELIVER SUPPLIES AND FUEL TO U.S. TROOPS.

PARARESCUE TEAMS ARE TRAINED TO WORK TOGETHER TO PROVIDE THE BEST CARE FOR THEIR PATIENTS.

THE FIRST PJs

In 1943, during the height of World War II, a group of airmen needed to be rescued after they parachuted out of their plane before it crashed near the border between China and Burma (Myanmar). This was the first U.S. pararescue mission.

The downed airmen were in a jungle far away from any roads or trails. The only way to reach them was by parachute. Lieutenant Colonel Don Flickinger and two medical specialists parachuted into the jungle to locate the airmen and treat their injuries. The group was led out of the jungle to safety more than a month later.

LIEUTENANT COLONEL FLICKINGER AND
THE MEDICS WITH HIM FACED MANY
PROBLEMS BESIDES LOCATING THE
AIRMEN AND TREATING THEIR INJURIES.
SOME FRIENDLY LOCAL PEOPLE HELPED
THE U.S. AIRMEN.

PARARESCUE MISSIONS

After World War II, pararescue units continued to aid the U.S. military in other conflicts. They served bravely in both the Korean War and the Vietnam War.

During the Vietnam War, PJs used helicopters to complete their missions. This was dangerous because enemy soldiers often shot at helicopters while they were **hovering**. Much of the Vietnam War was fought in the jungle. Helicopters were able to hover over injured soldiers so pararescue units could safely drop to them. PJs used cables to lower themselves to the ground to take care of soldiers' injuries. Then PJs and injured soldiers were pulled up to the helicopter.

ASTRONAUT RESCUE!

IN 1966, THE GEMINI 8 MISSION TEAM WAS FORCED
TO LAND THEIR SPACECRAFT IN THE PACIFIC OCEAN.
PJs USED SPECIAL EQUIPMENT TO HELP THE SPACECRAFT
STAY AFLOAT UNTIL A NAVY SHIP COULD ARRIVE TO PICK
UP THE ASTRONAUTS AND THE PJs.

DURING THE VIETNAM WAR, THE U.S. AIR FORCE USED
C-123 PROVIDER AIRCRAFT, ONE OF WHICH IS SHOWN
HERE, TO DROP TROOPS OFF, DELIVER SUPPLIES, AND
RESCUE INJURED SOLDIERS.

11

In the early 1990s, pararescue forces saved airmen during the Gulf War. U.S. Air Force troops were a big part of this operation against Iraq. They bombed the enemy and carried supplies. The PJs used helicopters again during their missions to find and treat downed pilots and wounded airmen.

Pararescue units also rescue people who are in trouble outside of war zones. They helped many people after a 1989 earthquake in San Francisco, California, and after Hurricane Katrina hit the Gulf Coast in 2005. After a terrible earthquake in Haiti in 2010, PJs and similar teams from many other countries helped bring aid to people who needed it.

IN 2011, A PARARESCUE TEAM FROM KIRTLAND AIR FORCE BASE SEARCHED A MOUNTAINOUS AREA OF COLORADO FOR A MISSING HIKER. SHE HAD BEEN LOST FOR TWO DAYS WHEN PARARESCUEMEN USED A HELICOPTER TO RESCUE HER.

13

TRAINING TO BECOME A PJ

Airmen who want to begin pararescue training must first pass the Physical Ability and **Stamina** Test (PAST). This is a tough physical test that candidates must be able to complete in three hours or less. Airmen are expected to swim, run, and do physically tiring exercises. Not all airmen can pass this test.

A PJ candidate must be in top physical shape to begin training, but he must also meet other requirements. As of 2016, all special ops positions are open to women. However, only men have passed through pararescue training as of the printinng of this book. PJ candidates must be high school graduates. PJs must be U.S. citizens. Finally, they must be able to see really well too.

PAST REQUIREMENTS

PAST BEGINS WITH BASIC EXERCISES: AT LEAST EIGHT PULL-UPS IN TWO MINUTES, AT LEAST 50 SIT-UPS IN TWO MINUTES, AND AT LEAST 40 PUSH-UPS IN TWO MINUTES. AFTER A 10-MINUTE REST, CANDIDATES MUST COMPLETE A 1.5-MILE (2.4 KM) RUN IN UNDER 10 MINUTES AND 20 SECONDS. AFTER A 30-MINUTE REST, CANDIDATES MUST THEN COMPLETE TWO UNDERWATER SWIMS OF 82 FEET (25 M), AND FINISH WITH A 0.3-MILE (500 M) SWIM IN UNDER 15 MINUTES.

DO YOU HAVE WHAT IT TAKES TO ENTER PJ TRAINING? IT'S NOT EASY!

15

If an airman passes the PAST test, they next report to Lackland Air Force Base in Texas for the Pararescue Preparatory Course and the **Indoctrination** Course. For three months, they train hard and learn many skills, such as using medical terms and exercising leadership, all of which help them in later training.

Next, PJ candidates attend the U.S. Army Airborne School at Fort Benning, Georgia. There, they learn the basics of parachuting. Each soldier must complete five parachute jumps. Two jumps are during the day with just a parachute and **reserve parachute**. Three jumps are in full battle gear. Two of these are during the day. The final jump is at night. Those who pass earn the honor to wear the maroon beret.

MAROON BERET

PARARESCUE SPECIAL OPS AIRMEN ARE THE ONLY GROUP IN THE U.S. MILITARY THAT'S ALLOWED TO WEAR THE MAROON BERET. IT'S A MARK OF HONOR.

17

Training isn't over yet. PJ trainees travel to U.S. Air Force Combat Diver School in Panama City, Florida. There, they spend six weeks learning how to use different kinds of diving equipment. They also learn how to use that equipment to sneak into areas controlled by the enemy and search for downed airmen. They practice these skills in water up to 130 feet (40 m) deep!

After this, they attend the U.S. Navy Underwater **Egress** Training. This one-day course teaches soldiers how to safely escape from an aircraft that has crashed and is sinking into water.

SURVIVAL

NEXT, TRAINEES TRAVEL TO U.S. AIR FORCE BASIC
SURVIVAL SCHOOL AT FAIRCHILD AIR FORCE BASE IN
WASHINGTON STATE. FOR 19 DAYS, TRAINEES LEARN
HOW TO SURVIVE IN ANY ENVIRONMENT AND HOW TO
FIND THEIR WAY TO SAFETY.

UNDERWATER EGRESS TRAINING
TAKES PLACE AT PENSACOLA NAVAL
AIR STATION IN FLORIDA.

ADVANCED PARACHUTING

Basic parachute training simply isn't enough for pararescue. After survival school in Washington, trainees go to Freefall Parachutist School at Fort Bragg, North Carolina. There, trainees learn special parachuting skills, such as air **maneuvers** and how to handle free fall, or the part of the parachute drop before the parachute opens.

Trainees then go to the Yuma Proving Grounds in Arizona where they learn even more advanced parachutist skills. This facility features a **wind tunnel** for specialized training in a safe environment. Trainees then practice both day and night drops as well as jumping at high and low **altitudes**.

MEDICAL TRAINING

IN ADDITION TO PARACHUTE AND SURVIVAL TRAINING,
TRAINEES GO TO THE 22-WEEK PARAMEDIC COURSE TO
LEARN HOW TO PROVIDE EMERGENCY MEDICAL TREATMENT.
NEXT, THE PJs ATTEND THE PARARESCUE RECOVERY
SPECIALIST COURSE IN NEW MEXICO FOR 24 WEEKS.
THEY PRACTICE RESCUES USING A HELICOPTER AND
LEARN TO GIVE MEDICAL CARE IN THE FIELD.

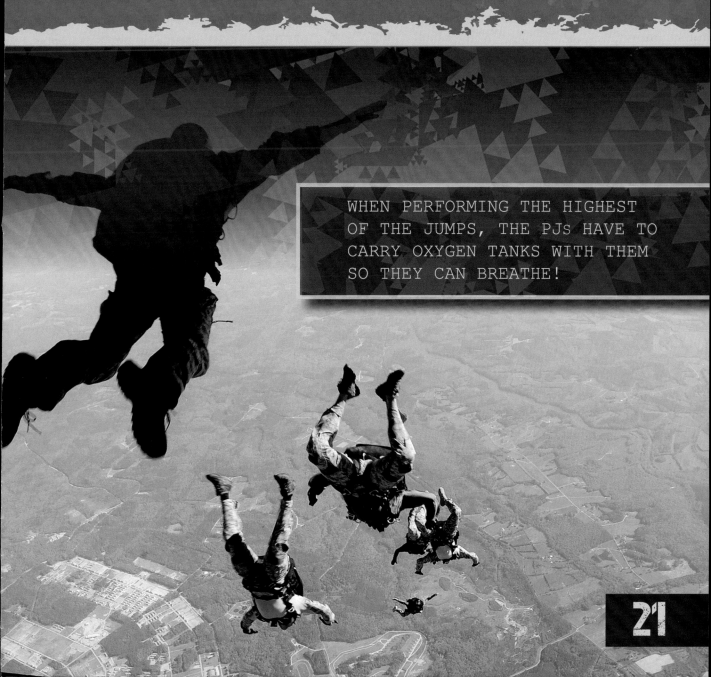

WHEN PERFORMING THE HIGHEST
OF THE JUMPS, THE PJs HAVE TO
CARRY OXYGEN TANKS WITH THEM
SO THEY CAN BREATHE!

While training at Yuma, PJs learn HALO parachuting and HAHO parachuting. "HALO" stands for high-altitude, low-opening. A HALO jump starts at 35,000 feet (10.67 km), but the PJ doesn't open his parachute until he's only 2,500 feet (762 m) above the ground. This makes it harder for an enemy to detect a PJ because he's traveling very fast for most of his drop.

"HAHO" stands for high-altitude, high-opening. PJs jump from aircraft flying up to 35,000 feet (10.67 km) and open their parachutes after only a few seconds of free fall. PJs float down quietly. They're often able to drift behind enemy lines undetected.

PJs CARRY A SPECIAL
MACHINE ON THEIR
PARACHUTES THAT OPEN
THEM WHEN THEY REACH
THE RIGHT ALTITUDE.

23

TOOLS OF
THE TRADE

Pararescue teams rely on high-tech tools and vehicles to complete their missions. Rescue helicopters were first used in World War II. These large helicopters, commonly called "Jolly Green Giants," carried injured soldiers on stretchers to safety. As helicopter technology improved, PJs had access to faster helicopters that could carry more passengers for greater distances.

Today, pararescue teams use the MV-22 Osprey, which is a tilt-rotor aircraft. This means that the pilot can change the position of the rotors, which are the parts that make the aircraft fly. The Osprey can fly long distances like an airplane. It can also take off and land quickly like a helicopter.

RESCUE ALL-TERRAIN TRANSPORT

ONCE ON THE GROUND, PJs RELY ON THE RESCUE ALL-**TERRAIN** TRANSPORT (RATT) TO GET AROUND. RATTs ARE DROPPED FROM AIRCRAFT WITH PARACHUTES. EACH RATT CAN CARRY TWO PJs AND UP TO SIX PATIENTS. RATTs ARE EQUIPPED WITH MEDICAL SUPPLIES SO PJs CAN TREAT INJURIES ON THE MOVE.

PJS CARRY A PACK FULL OF MEDICAL SUPPLIES TO TREAT THEIR PATIENTS. THEY ALSO NEED NIGHT-VISION GOGGLES TO HELP THEM SEE IN THE DARK ON NIGHT MISSIONS. PJs ALSO CARRY GUNS.

CHIEF MASTER SERGEANT DUANE HACKNEY

Duane Hackney is remembered as the bravest PJ in the history of the U.S. Air Force. Hackney went on more than 200 search-and-rescue missions during the Vietnam War. During one mission, Hackney and a rescued pilot boarded a helicopter that was soon struck by enemy fire. The explosion blew Hackney out of the helicopter. He opened his chute but still fell roughly to the ground. After, Hackney returned to the downed helicopter to find the rest of the crew had died.

Hackney remained in pararescue until he retired as a chief master sergeant in 1991. During that time, he earned more than 70 awards, including an Air Force Cross and two Purple Hearts.

DECORATED HERO

DUANE HACKNEY WAS THE FIRST LIVING AIRMAN TO RECEIVE THE AIR FORCE CROSS, WHICH IS AWARDED TO U.S. AIR FORCE AIRMEN FOR **EXTRAORDINARY** HEROISM. THE PURPLE HEART IS AWARDED TO SOLDIERS WHO WERE INJURED OR KILLED IN BATTLE. HACKNEY ALSO EARNED A SILVER STAR (FOR **VALOR** IN COMBAT), FOUR **DISTINGUISHED** FLYING CROSSES (FOR HEROISM OR EXTRAORDINARY ACHIEVEMENT DURING AN AERIAL FLIGHT), AND 18 AIR MEDALS (A LESSER VERSION OF THE DISTINGUISHED FLYING CROSS).

DURING THE VIETNAM WAR, HACKNEY HELPED DELIVER TWINS IN A LOCAL VILLAGE! HE ALSO SAVED A LOCAL FAMILY TRAPPED IN A BURNING HUT.

27

"THAT OTHERS MAY LIVE"

On each PJ's maroon beret is a flash, or small patch, displaying the pararescue motto, "That Others May Live." It shows a picture of a parachute above a guardian angel wrapping its arms around the world. This shows the PJs' commitment to saving other peoples' lives even in dangerous situations.

Today, U.S. Air Force pararescue teams continue to support U.S. military actions all over the world. They give medical aid to those who need it and perform rescue missions for soldiers and U.S. citizens alike. These brave soldiers put their own lives at risk in order to save others.

GLOSSARY

altitude: The height of something, such as an airplane, above sea level.

cyberspace: The online world of computer networks and especially the internet.

distinguished: Marked by excellence.

egress: Having to do with coming out of or exiting something.

extraordinary: Very good or impressive.

hover: To float in the air without moving in any direction.

indoctrination: The act of teaching the ideas, opinions, or beliefs of a certain group.

maneuver: A planned movement done in a careful or skillful way.

reserve parachute: An additional parachute in case the main parachute fails to work properly.

stamina: The ability or strength to keep doing something for a long time.

terrain: A type of land.

valor: Courage or bravery.

wind tunnel: A long, narrow room through which air is blown in order to test the effects of wind on an airplane, human being, or other object.

FOR MORE INFORMATION

BOOKS

Murray, Julie. *Air Force Pararescue*. Mendota Heights, MN: North Star Editions, 2020.

Slater, Lee. *Pararescue Jumpers*. Minneapolis, MN: ABDO Publishing, 2015.

WEBSITES

Pararescue

www.airforce.com/careers/detail/pararescue
Learn much more about pararescue from the official U.S. Air Force website.

Air Force Pararescue

www.operationmilitarykids.org/air-force-pararescue-pjs/
Read more about what it takes to become a PJ.

Publisher's note to educators and parents: Our editors have carefully reviewed these websites to ensure that they are suitable for students. Many websites change frequently, however, and we cannot guarantee that a site's future contents will continue to meet our high standards of quality and educational value. Be advised that students should be closely supervised whenever they access the internet.

INDEX